Voyage To The Secret Love

Madhumita Dutta

BookLeaf Publishing
India | USA | UK

Presentation by *BookLeaf Publishing*

Web: www.bookleafpub.com

E-mail: info@bookleafpub.com

ISBN: 9789360942090

First edition 2024

In loving memory of my father

(Late) Mr Mahitosh Dutta, my first Guru.

ACKNOWLEDGEMENT

Voyage To The Secret Love is every traveller's story. As human beings, we all have travelled near and far. While we travel, we sometimes meet souls who stay in our hearts forever. This book is a story of those emotions that we experience in our journey through life. Poems are compositions that give us bliss, take us back down memory lane and our mind travels from present to past and imagines the future.

This book is a reality because of writer-friendly forums like BookLeaf. I have to especially thank my husband, with whom I have travelled across the world. The experiences that I have in life are because of him. He has been my companion for a lifetime. I'm grateful to my parents, son, brother and friends who have been encouraging me to write. They have shown immense faith in me and that has been my motivation. I earnestly hope that my poems will take the readers through a kaleidoscope of emotions through the prism of travel.

PREFACE

When we travel, we are liberated as we are open to all kinds of emotions, just like a child. As we grow in life, we draw a boundary around us and hinder people from entering our souls. But as adults, when we travel, we experience love, joy, nostalgia, heartbreak, and grief and when the vacation is over, we rejoin our normal lives. However, during those few days when we were close to nature, our fantasies and horizons widened. Our souls witnessed emotions that would help us survive in life. Globetrotter's journey is one where she fell in love with nature and souls who reminded her of childhood, teenage, college life and her past life. Nature speaks to her, flirts with her and is her best friend who has been with her always. Nature brought her close to her secret love.

The Northern Lights

Fleeting leaves
Chilly wind
Streamy wave
And they went
To the caves
Saw the stalagmites
Went deeper
Along the turquoise stream...
Through the whole...
They witnessed the starry night
Painted with northern lights...
Green and Red...
Ready to Wed.

Banana Leaf

It was dark
And the sky roared...
The leaves were twirling
With the wind
It started drizzling...
She stood beneath
A banana leaf
As the lightning flashed
She saw him all washed...
Both were drenched
And the thirst quenched...
They held the banana leaf.
And walked in the rain
Love showered,
Like never again.

North Star

Between Heaven and Earth...
I feel your warmth...
Especially in the north...
Where the star shines...
I know it's mine.

Marsedenia of Madagascar

As the night grows
Darkness dawns...
And the whites are visible
Sitting over the Baobab...
He witnesses nature's show...
Sparkling star
Near and far...
Glittering white algae
Moving in a rally...
Marsedenia's glow...
Made his heart flow...
And He danced to the tune...
Of Moon
Suddenly came a fairy
And the night became merry.

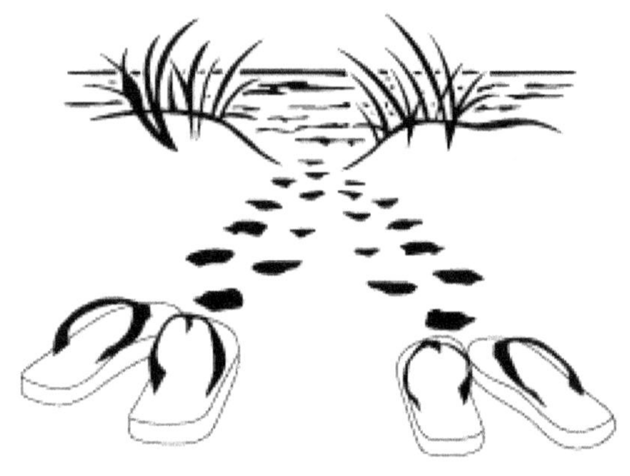

Romance de Etretat

The clouds unveiled
And the Sun was revealed...
Rays on the sea...
Sparkling waves...
View through the caves...
Me and you...
Holding hands...
Footprints on sand
And made love so grand.

Aurora's Dance in Lofoten

Rustling leaves...
Peeping owl...
Little fireflies...
Dark night...
Glittering sky
She said, 'Hi'
To the stars.
'Why so far'
The wind is playing guitar
The Sky turned
Green, red and purple
All in a circle...
She saw aurora
Amidst natural flora.
They danced...
In mystical aura.

Tete-e-Tete

Morning hues...
You and me...
Sipping tea...
Chirping birds
On the tree.

Turquoise Blue

Eloquent birds...
Tweeting words...
Fragile bond...
A magical wand
Sometimes broken
The essence is taken...
Love once gone...
Never comes back...
In the same flavour
Yes, there is charm
And He is warm...
Nature's spell…
In calmness of the shell…
Made a fairytale...

Land of Fire and Ice

She was lost
To never come back...
As everything...
Turned black...
She was seeking green...
Found an island so serene...
She wished to star
Chatted with the sea
Rested on the trees...
Then came the wind...
Got on his knees...
Said, 'Let's go overseas'.
While flying,
She saw the Island
So black
It was emotion
Which he lacked...
He was alone.
In his black throne.

A Date With Sky

I'm going on a date with Sky...
It follows me everywhere...
It showers rain when I'm sad...
It teases me with a leaf...
He is real...
That's my belief.

Bougainvilleas of Arizona

She was visiting Arizona
Splashed with Bougainvillaeas...
Pink and white...
On an evening sky...
Standing in the square...
He placed it on her hair.
And it was a dreamy affair.

In The Land of Windmill

Wild berries
Makes me merry
The birds are humming,
And berries are blossoming.

Siamese Smile

In the land of lotus
We found us...
Kayaking through the mangroves...
We reached the Lot Caves...
And I saw him wave...
He was a stranger...
Yet he smiled...
I was amazed...
As we dived into the sea...
He came closer to me...
Placed my hand...
On his heart...
And said, 'Love is an art'.
I thank God...
That you are true...
Loving you is now my virtue.

Cherry Blossom

Cherry Blossom
She is here...
And when he winks...
She places a kiss
With petals so pink...
She is all he thinks.

Promenade in Orang

On her night promenade...
In the wilderness...
She looked for him...
In the dark...
And saw a spark...
As she moved near...
The fog whispered in her ear...
'Follow the leaves'.
And hope weaved...
She entered the cave...
There was water and wave...
He stood there...
And said, 'Let go,
As I'm in a different realm of time...
Seasons flow,
So will your tears...
This cave was dry...
Your tears brought water
Your smile makes the flowers bloom...
Your heart makes my heart beat...
So retreat...
As it's not your time'.
She opened her eyes...
And saw fireflies...
All was dark yet bright...
Made him vanish in the mist...
And the leaves kissed.

Sunset by The Lighthouse

I wish it was forever
With no beginning
And end...

The Lighthouse was our place...
Where saw the sea
The clouds
The Horizon...
For the first time...
Our first kiss...
Immersed in rain...
Then came the twister...
And the sea called you...
For rescue...
Since then,
Every evening I walk till the end...
And wait till sunset...
He rowed through the waves...
And reached the shore...
Looking into my eyes, said,
'I love you more, more and more'.

My heart knew then...
I was forever
With no beginning
No end...

In Frozen Land With Frozen Heart...

In frozen land...
With Frozen heart...
She saw him...
After ten years...
Out of nowhere...
He stood there...
And was starring...
Once she fell for those eyes...
But now there are no ties...
Before, his presence
Would give her butterflies
To her heart, he was a stranger...
And that was a surprise...
Love is frozen...
And their knot is broken...
It was not meant to be...
She was happy and free...
In frozen land...
She flew with a warm heart...
Over the white desert.

Lost in Lofoten

Behind the veil of Darkness
Night descended...
In Leknes...
She found the green sky...
Dancing
And romancing...
With her eyes...
Where lies...
The darkness of Ocean
And the light of ice.
Love of cold...
Yet nice...

Italy
VENICE

Lost in Venice

Strolling by the Grand Canal...
She walked into a cafe...
Sipping the coffee...
She knew it was her day...
As he came by to sit
And stay...
They wandered in the zigzag way...
Love was in sway...
As Cupid shoot an arrow
They found romance and sorrow...

Flirty Queen

She is the queen...
Pink on Green...
She was here to win
But got lost...
In frost...
He emerged...
Amidst the ocean
From the Fire and Ice Nation
They got lost again
In rain
Love was a mystery
They weaved an unknown tapestry.

Orange Sky

It's time
To let go
It's time
To come back
To those blue sky
Which has turned orange
As nothing has changed,
It's been a while,
That I have seen you smile.
On the cosy winter evening
The stars are twinning.
So, I'm here...
To call you back...
To the universe
Of love.
It's time to let go
Let your heart flow...

A Tomorrow with You

Life goes on
Even if there is no star in the sky
Life goes on
Even if he forgot, it was our date night
Life goes on
Because I have given you tomorrow
As you lost me today
And if you lose me tomorrow
I'll wait until the day after
Life goes on
Come soon

Mirabilis of Peru

In the foothills of the Andes
He found Mirabilis
So pink...
Floating on a leaf
In the river Magdalena...
That evening
He saw her across the wood
She was like a miracle
They laughed, cried and hugged
It was dawn
He saw Mirabilis on the leaf
Flowing on Magdalena
Found her ballerina
Waited for the night to fall
And it was love
Once and for all...

A Blue Sky in Ukraine

I woke up and could see
Fumes all around
The sky was grey
All I could do was pray
I left my house
I left my son
I left my love
So, I pray that tomorrow I wake up and see
A blue sky
With a rising Ukraine
Standing up strong again

A Rainy Evening in Mandalay

Strolling through the moist Irrawaddy forest
He thought of her
Love means
Her heartbeat
Her one look
This evening
When it rained
She was in the swing
Gliding through
He offered her the umbrella
But in vain
As she was immersed in the rain
And when they walked
Holding hands
Drenched
Time stopped
To see their romance
But their soul was in a trance.

Monsoon Wedding

As the wind blows
The petals fall
To die
But to live again
In the next rain
Looking at the sky
Telling its love story,
Petal says,
'Tree, don't you worry
Next rain we will marry.
Now, Mother Earth is ready
To embrace us
As we all are precious'.

Being Unknown in Hallstatt

And I'm lost
In time
In my mind
In nature
In you
What if I don't want to be rescued?
Being lost
Is my dream
Where I'm family to everyone
Where everyone is mine
My name is unknown
But still, they call me,
'Hyacinth of Hallstatt'.

A Date In Bali

The sky proposed to me
In my last birth
In Bali
But I said, 'No'
This time
He was wise
Gave me a bunch of Jepuns thrice
And I said, 'Qui'
As I love the way he loves me
He follows me everywhere
Showers me with rain
Teases me with wind
Wipes my tears with leaves
He holds my hand
And the waves whispered
'I'm here, near and everywhere'.

Crystals on Pine

She was the girl with the green hat
The coniferous lover
She sat amidst the pine
Sipped her wine
Spoke to the trees
And forgot her miseries
Then came the snow
With glittering crystals on the leaves below
Reminded her that she was here
A long time ago
With him
As she looked up
He popped
Out of the tree
She set him free
He said, 'Ask as you wish'
She said, 'One kiss'
They kissed for hours
And that was love's power
He left her a ring
And disappeared in the mist.

Walking Through the Valley of Rudraksh

Walking through the sleepy lanes of Nepal
She was searching for a fruit
She asked the mountains,
The waterfalls,
The river,
The trees
No one knew
Where it grew
She slept amidst the willow
Past midnight
She saw two huge feet
Walking through the blue hill
She followed her will
Saw the hills opening
It was a light which flashed out
She opened her eyes
And it was morning
She felt something warm
In her palm
It was a rudraksh
Bright and brown
It resembled the universe
She held it between her fingers
And it conversed
About the deity,
Shiva the almighty

Tears by the Volga

I stand on the cloud
And see the world beneath
I see you by the Volga river
Every night when you sit and weep
And remember me
I cry too
Tears drop as dew
Every day is new
But there is no one like you
Our evening tea together
Our star gazing nights
Our weaving of dreams
I miss everything
I wish I had a wing
To fly to you and sing
Lullaby and put you to sleep
Tears roll down
As you close eyes
Slowly the tears dry
Forget me
At least try.

Love in Airport

She sat beside me
And I thought that
It will be a lovely journey
Destiny struck
And her seat got changed
My golden opportunity was lost
But I didn't give up
As she moved away
I convinced destiny
And sat with her again
As the flight flew
Everything felt new
The clouds
The stars
The sky
All were rejoicing
I don't know why
Those two hours
Seemed forever
Every time she turned her face
I saw those
Twinkling eyes
Windy hair
And then the plane landed
This wasn't fair
It was an adieu
She turned back
And said, 'Thank you'.

The City of Joy

I visited our city of joy
Our city
Where you taught me
To walk
To talk
To stand bravely against all odds
To embrace happiness
To have faith
But now when I stand by Hoogly river
I don't find you beside me
Everything seems empty
Your wholehearted love
Is what I miss
I'm lonely in this crowd
Where everyone is running fast
To be in the race
But I paused
And my heart went into a flashback
Our first ride in a car
Our first dance at home
My first job and your hug
My first trophy and your smile
My tears and your heartbeat
Standing by the Hoogly River
I can say no one loved me more than you
In my next birth, if I have a father it should be
you.

Love in Atlantis

I loved you when we were together
I love you when we are apart
I love you in your silence
In the ocean of life
We are sailing in different ships
Mine is happiness
Yours is success
Love stays
So, have you
In my being
Even today when I see a lotus
It reminds me of us
But I feel someday
When we both would be tired
And our ships sink
We will reunite in Atlantis
Deep down in the ocean
And express our emotion
Of love and hate
As we are not ideal mates.

Love in Agra

When I knew love
I started looking for you
Everywhere
Then, after 24 years, we met
It seemed to be fate
My heart discovered
You in me
And me in you.

SPAIN

Miranda de Ebro

Every time you bid adieu
It rains.
We met in Spain
By the river Ebro
It was spring
Yet it rained
We sauntered into the streets
Of Miranda de Ebro
Holding the umbrella
Our world inside
Seemed cosy and warm
Your heart crossed mine
By then it was nine
Night fell
Yet we had endless stories to tell
But it was time to bid farewell
The sky had tears
And there was a heavy shower
Even in the last hour
You left a flower
Which is still near
And dear
To me
As I sail in the sea.

Love Story on A Maple Leaf

Last evening
She sat beside the maple tree
It's autumn
Red, yellow and orange were all over
Enmeshed in each other
With each falling maple leaf
Falls her love
It lies down on earth
Looking at the sky above
Wishing to stay
But the sky believes
It is the day
To tell
Her love story
Simple yet full of glory
She wrote her story
On the maple leaf
The wind took it
And smeared the air
With the fragrance of romance
That's why it is said, 'Love is in the air'.

Rise of Shakti on Earth

She is here to tell
The story of nature
To give voice to her soul
To stand by the oppressed
To give happiness to the depressed
She is here to love
And be loved
She is here to witness
The marriage of the Sun and the Moon
Every dawn, dusk and noon
She is the wisdom
Of fire, water and earth
She will lead the path
To destroy the demon,
Who pretend to be uncommon
So, rise to your thought
And conscience
Let the emotions flow
The world has become cold
And everywhere there is snow
The day will come soon
When truth will rise
And there will be a new Sun
In your eyes.

Yellow Lanes

Yellow lanes
Live and dream
As seasons flow
Fleeting winds make the petals blow
Red and yellow
As it is time
For them to go
Immersed in nature's lap
After a short nap
Only to come back.

Love Happened

Love happened
When you looked at me
Through the binoculars
From the window pane
Love happened
When you sat beside me in school
Love happened
When we danced on the prom night
And you held me tight
Love happened
When I smiled and you ignored me
As I was awestruck at your smile
Love happened
When you left for the city
And I used to miss your eyes so pretty
Love happened
When I was alone
With you not being around
Everyone seems unknown
But I live today
To live the moment we lived together
To die to the moment when we were apart
Love happens and it happens in every moment
Since the day we met
Love stayed.

Love is feather

I left your lane
Where we walked till late at night
Watching the stars and moon
I left your lane
Where I stood for hours
To get a glimpse of yours
I left when you left me
But I still live
To the moments
Of laughter and tears
That we shared for years
Love is a feather
Which I wear proudly
Forever

When They Met in Burnpur

Though he liked her
Since the first day
But he pretended to ignore
Yet she promised to love him more
As they were in their teens
She proposed to her amidst the greens
And this was his dream
Love blossomed
But with an overcast
Their relationship became a thing of the past
After several years
He came with a surprise
To give her a hug
And to get her back
It was new year
She was dancing with her mom
He took her aside
And told the magical word
She said, 'Yes'
And life became fun
They ran to the horizons of the Moon and the
Sun.
The love birds of Burnpur
Finally became one.

Blue Hazels of Austria and Him

I was travelling
Through the countryside
Found blue hazels all over the meadows
Rustic and mellow
As the train stopped
In Obertraun
A man with a big hat
Sat opposite to me
I ignored
Yet I cared
When I gazed at him
From the corner of my eyes
His eyes were like blue hazels
Glittering the sea
And I thought me and him
Can be 'We'
It was morning
Still, his eyes were what I was adorning
Our journey ended
In silence
As I was getting down from the train
He offered his hand
Walked till the end of the lane
To my surprise
He turned out to be wise
While bidding farewell
He presented me with a bunch of blue hazel.

tea

Over a Cup of Tea

In misty tea gardens
We strolled
And spoke about life
As afternoon became dusk
We tasted our tea
From ginger lemon to chamomile
It was worthwhile
As dusk became night
Clouds descended
And our journey ended
With a kiss
Venturing into the world of strangers
Your friendship is pure bliss
Meet you again
Till my next wish.

Twin Souls

And it was the Cherry Blossom
Which showered the pink hue
Pines were few
But leaves were old and new
They are my twin souls
It was heartbreaking to bid them adieu
As we never knew
When we would meet again
But we are tied in a chain
Of bond
Of love
Of hope
That we will meet again in the same globe
As it is a believe
We are entwined in the same weave.

He left Daisy

When I woke up to live my dreams
I saw these little daisies
That you left last night
And everything felt right
Those little white pearls
Reminded him of snow on my curls
In college I became the daisy girl
Who fell in love with an Earl.

Let the Doors Be Open

94

Let the doors be open
For the wind
To blow out the dust
Let the doors be open
For you to walk into the world
Where the known becomes unknown
And the unknown becomes known.

Memories in Balconies

Balconies are special
As we see the world ahead
From the balcony
Which is our home
The morning blue sky
The birds passing by
The sunrise and sunset
The rain that made us wet
Our coffee night
And clouds misty white
The star gazing
With a smile so amusing
Balconies give us memories
And takes our worries
It is the cosy corner
Where hugs are warmer
Balconies are special
As it is where love nestles.

Beneath The Lemon Tree

You and me were 'Just Friends'.
Our first rendezvous
Was beneath the lemon tree
Where we smelled the aroma
Of being free
Seasons changed
The leaves fell
But the aroma was there
And love was in the air
Our hearts didn't care
As we thought our friendship
Was there to stay
And it can't be any other way
Life is fate
To our surprise
We were not the best mates
Wind blew the aroma
To the sky
And today we are alone
We don't know why?
But the lemon tree
Is present
Showering its scent
As I smell it today
I think our friendship
Lies in our heart
Memories can never fall apart.
You and me were 'Just Friends'
And we will just be.

Masquerade Night

It was time
For the masquerade
Of Nature
The clouds descended
The trees became the audience
Then came the Queen and the King
In butterfly's wing
It was a ball
But a secret one
As royals
They could never
Hold hands
Or tap their feet
Or
Place a kiss
Night is boundless
So are they
Love found a new way.
She sat and witnessed
Nature's play.

REEL SHARED ON SEP 5, 2024

BY @MADHU.MITA_777